FARTING PRESIDENTS
AND OTHER POEMS

POEMS

GW00696131

992312301 4

Kraftgriots

Also in the series (POETRY)

FARTING PRESIDENTS
AND OTHER POEMS

POEMS

'Tope Omoniyi

kraftgriots

Published by

Kraft Books Limited
6A Polytechnic Road, Sango, Ibadan
Box 22084, University of Ibadan Post Office
Ibadan, Oyo State, Nigeria
℡ 234 (02) 8106655
E-mail: krabooks@skannet.com
steyrhill@usa.net

© 'Tope Omoniyi 2001

First published 2001

ISBN 978–039–043–X

= KRAFTGRIOTS =
(A literary imprint of Kraft Books Limited)

All Rights Reserved

First printing, July 2001

Computer typeset by MOWA Computers, Ibadan

Printmarks Ventures, Ososami, Ibadan.

For baba and mama, Folorunso and Omorinola

... in time, the nursery rhymes and folk tales of infancy
inspire our art and vision to paint wordscapes
of farting presidents who shred the grace of office
with gunshots from the arse in private and public spaces

Gloucestershire County Library

992312301 4	
Askews	13-Nov-2002
	£6.95

Acknowledgement

Some poems in this collection have been previously published either in a journal or an anthology and I specifically acknowledge the following in accordance with copyright provisions:

— (1995) 'A letter to Cyril in Indianapolis' in Mikkelson, Shirley (ed.) *Echoes from the silence*. Vol. 1, Harlingen, TX: Quill Books.

— (1996) 'Every Day' in *Tenggara: Journal of Southeast Asian Literature*, Vol. 38, Kuala Lumpur: Universiti Kebangsaan, Malaysia.

— (1998) 'Goldfish and watersnail' and 'Vanity Rose' in *The Gombak Review: A Biannual of Creative Writing and Critical Comment*, Vol. 3:1, Selangor: International Islamic University, Malaysia.

— (2000) 'Clouds' in Hoskins, J., Westwood, M. and Sawers, G. (eds.) *The Unruly Sun*, Vol. 5, Reading: The Rising Sun Arts Centre.

ANA Review published some others in 1997. I wish to thank Drew Tombrello for producing and directing *Sky High* as a dramatic patchwork from a selection of poems in this volume and ESSO for sponsoring it under the Arts Hour Scheme at the National Institute of Education, Singapore in March 1997.

Contents

Let them who have ears hear

feed them from fibres of history
on the graveless end of tyrants

teach them from signs of the times
that these are not rumours and murmurs
but the war cries of distressed gods
targeting bullet vendors
and two-kobo Generals

let them who have ears hear
in the barracks and Government House
that only dogs destined to stray
defy the hunter's rally

those who wrestle with the gods
contend with the Unseen
the Mighty Sigidi, spirit warrior
making a mockery of letter bombs
and tanks

for a nation on cliff-edge
only a half-tilt will quench the appetite
of angry gods
the mightiest will fall to a pulp
commoners will stretch their creases
and wait for coronation next season.

The politics of silence

nothing

nothing

nothing happens,
so nothing changes,
just silence
into

nothing.

simply living,
every breath a death
commemorates
your demise
in silent instalments.

I do not know anymore

I do not know what to do with the elders of my clan
I do not know what to make of their pacifism
all night long they preach a gospel of non-violence
but they hang at dawn
and are buried at noon

I do not know what to do about the rage in my veins
I do not know what to make of this rebel urge
all night long I hatch plans of assault against the enemy
then bow to elderly wisdom
and carry coffins

I do not know what to do anymore
to rouse the world
I do not know how to mould
their bashful threats into bombs
all night long they warn these sons of a gun
but daybreak serenades an unholy swoon
and raises a toast to enemies of our moon

I do not know anything anymore
but for one — we're a tribe of warriors
when my time comes
my crimson stream will join the ritual flow
    I shall embrace their gallows with a smile
    and a prayer that our passing bring
    strength and defiance to pall bearers.

Every day

every day
    a small peep
    in the sky
    for a message
    from the gods
every day
    a peer into
    the heart
    for where
    this road
    leads
every day
    i wait
    patiently
    for barred gates
      of the sky
      the shrine
      to open
      and feed
      my waiting
every day
    i wonder
    curiously
    if i chase
      another's god
      and walk
      another's road
    peeping and peering.

No thirst is quenched

raise a glass to thirst
you who have water
and philosophise

who talks of measured steps
to harsh rhythms
the drumbeats of hunger?

for this is a season
of apocalyptic dance,
concert of cursed contortions

who bakes the crumbs
to feed continents of beggars
that hide behind clichéd histories?

for such invidious deed
wrecks the sails of vessels
destined for future harbours

who will unmask masquerades
on International Monitoring Fronts
to expose New Age bondage?

for this is the propaganda
of infernal doles, slavery bonds
sold and bought North to South

and you who raise a glass know
that there is no dance
strung to empty stomachs
you who raise a glass know
that those who bake crumbs

insult the mast that unmasks
monitors of bondage

all who raise a glass know
that no thirst is quenched
by the sole-felt wetness
of waterless river-beds.

Fallen general

Your breath ran shivers down the spines of folks
And chilled the flow that made men men

Your strides left marks on the faces of women
Whose husbands you rammed

And dented the souls of husbands whose wives
You screwed for breaking your code of silence

Now I see you in the dock, epaulettes stripped
Metal clamps the jewellery you adorn

Across from you in the gallery
Folks who earnestly see justice
People once unfit for your presence
Have assigned their mandate to a judge

Embossed on their faces dignity
Unknown to chicken bully generals

Whose erection a gun sustains
But when the bullets melt like now
They whimper like anxious dogs

Now I see you in the dock images of simpletons
Invade my brain cells. You babble like babes
Without their innocence and stutter like rogues
Caught red-handed in their dreadful act

And I wonder endlessly how the hell
Chicken generals figured they could run a nation
From their DIY book of trash

Goldfish and watersnail

a goldfish is washed ashore
by a philandering river
caught in the web
of its own wandering

now the momentum
of its back-roll
cannot tame the weight
of gems in ripples

divested of its spirit
it flows back lifeless
cursed

a watersnail
is stranded on beach sand
the last current returned to sea
sober

goldfish and watersnail
wait for Judgement Day
both helpless
yet forever different.

Naked in the market-square

priests and princes have taken the floor
and i know that the times are doomed
this wriggling of priests and princes
not sanctified, unRoyal
far from these,
they dance in the nude
before the gaze of a thousand sockets
at the market-square

      so who guides
      and who needs a guard?
      for this game of striptease
undo the myth of prized offices
and none more may ever gape
in envy
we see now
that their crowns and cassocks are emblems
like licence in the hands of lawless drivers

naked our priests and princes dance
what then do we await
to know the revelations are now
and time's destination is round the corner
strange passions, strange persons
all tell tales of conclusion
for royalty and parsonage have taken the floor
naked in the market-square.

Yesterday's area boys

(For Wole Soyinka)

They have turned
statesmen

Countless epaulettes dress
their sleeves.

We shudder
in fearful admiration

the old siege is no longer confined
to the under-bridges of
Marina
close to midnight

The frontiers have extended
into the grounds of
Aso Rock

Tomorrow's children wail
in the nation's belly as
we light our candles
and pray to Allah,
whatever for!

Farting presidents

farting presidents go:
'ffffffffff'
'ffffffffffffffffff'
then steal a glance from
corner of eyes to see who's
cheeky enough to hold their breath

but noting smiles of understanding
despatched to save their faces,

farting presidents go:
'goooooof'
'gooooooooooooooofffffffffff'
then break their conference
with press, a pause
to see which journal reps.
wear mischief looks
threatening to leak the news
of leaks in presidential butts
again seeing no nerves
of dissent voices in sight

farting presidents go:
'fffffffffffffff'
'goooooooooooooooooooof'
'pooop, poooop, poopoooooooo'
easing pressure between
the clasps of cheeks
first in small puffs
of air endangering
then in gusts that rock
the boat of state
and noting that none
is yet uncalmed,

farting presidents go:
'ffff, gooof, poop, crap, crrrrraaaap'
slapping big fat craps across
the face of nation!

nothing sudden,
and i can swear, nothing
unexpected, for indeed
farting presidents test the waters
before they shit on the head of all

silence sends signals of consent
spare the rod and spoil the president!

Midwives or a deluge?

we have witnessed gross abominations
we have seen the castration of justice
on court-room slabs
we have swallowed fat frustrations
at the coronation of falsehood

    but now,
    gales and floods of cleansing
    or promises of them
    rip through our land
    parting anal feathers
    and exposing the foul frames

    of vicious uniformed contrivances!
    fixed forensic findings revealed
    vindicate victims of tutored miscarriage
    after the savaging in Ogoni
    fresh hunt now for stale villains
    royal victims craving judicial rebirth

but how long more
these gales and floods of cleansing?
how potent this royal injunction
for the burnishing of courtrooms?

our stables still fetid with mess
from unbriddled stallions on patrol
horrid stench of stillbirths
clench still to Wisdom Wigs

and so several yet languish
    for innocence
    perhaps in Kirikiri
    many more are hounded

in the streets and parks
in homes and pubs
from Benin to Birnin Kebbi

and as we approach the end
of our generation's tether
we wonder

if commissioned midwives can deliver us
from the miscarriage of Wigs and goons
and the tragic innocence of folks

or our stables must wait for a cleansing deluge?

Mongrel

I was four years old when grandpa began
to share his wisdom with us
my little brother jerry
and dainty sister siok and i.
grandpa spoke from a heavy tobacco chest.
each word its own breath claimed
this was our morning ritual
until he moved to the Rest House
the harbour from which they sail
to Godheartland we were told

grandpa taught us once
that those who dig for others' fall
erect the peak of their own free-fall.
the deeper the pit, the higher the height
from which they tumble.
grandpa didn't lie
for we have seen it played
on many a stage, jerry, siok and i

but my present puzzle stuns me
I see an old mongrel hollowing out graves
for cubs with eyes set on the future
and wonder if one grandpa
simply had no wisdom to share
or whether this mongrel
was an unlistening rascal in
her youth, and like the buffoons
of the French revolution
learned nothing and forgot nothing
stunned by the rising stake of her scoops,
and the shrine of mortal sacrifice below
I shudder with pity
my milk pod reaching out
to an undeserving mongrel.

We are uncast

you and i are uncast
in these fattening scenes
we roam the roads in search
and rake their trails for
fallen cowries and hardened crumbs
our streams are dry
we thirst
our fields are plain
we're famished
but we belch of overfeed
of hopes that tomorrow
our cocks shall crow
louder than theirs

not all is lost yet.

On listening to a BBC programme on the Spanish Revolution

it's Tuesday afternoon
in my long room, DIY cell.
radio voices re-enact the drama
of a big revolt in Spain.
they talk about Lorca and other poets,
singers whose daggers were sheathed
in verses of deadly words
they talk about those who fell
to Franco, their voices strike
hard and close home
in resemblance to here and now
as another revolution rages
in a centre concealed in my breath

the taming of a stubborn shrew
in Sister 'Franca',
upstairs' Chair with downstairs' brain
farting up the corridors
of my department.

i feel my rage,
i remember Lorca.
i cock my versified gun
with metaphors for bullets,
i lie in wait
to waste the waster,
in the Holy Book even the sins
of fathers can be visited
on the fourth generation
especially farting bullies'
heads.

Frontiers of anguish

birds of dusk dress Basra's skyline
but the ghosts of warlords
in silent whispers
mingle in the fields

a host of lost voices
stink in the wind.
on Basra's sands
stretches of the body-frames
of anguish tell tales of meddling
in a boiling crescent

in baghdad,
scudmaster sips a cocktail,
his toast to unconcluded rituals
and aborted sorties,
salted autobiographies polish off
the rough edges of dilatory commands
for retired generals and public servants
to ride the crest of desert storm
into Top Ten spots in P.O.Ps

in my soul,
i grieve for mothers
and sorrow for kids
of those in body-bags
their passage unaccounted
for in this hurried conclusions;
i mourn these perpetual sanctions
fuelling the toll daily
from ranks of people muted
by fear of Desert Vampire.

Tomorrow

Today we reek of royal defilement
And these rains are scanty
Forerunning showers strangled
But tomorrow the pores of heaven
Will open wide and we
Shall bathe with sainted sponges
We shall converge
And be submerged in cleansing flows
And when we resurface they'd be gone
Faeces and royalty in town council vans
Vanished at dawn for another donning.

New songs and sinful gods

my verse is silenced
they blind their ears to new songs
and strut to drumbeats of sinful gods,
rotted rhythms

but when my day dawns
they will be like water turtles washed ashore
by waves charged like their sinful gods,
frail, abandoned,
waves returned to sea,
sober, and they stand betrayed on sea-sand
even as i raise freshwater songs of hope
to console their tribe.

Rise poets, write

from farm house
to city street
from Kirikiri to Sabongari
from Nine-mile Corner
to Bonny
rise poets, write,

of silly heads in power
and several days of cower
rise poets, write,

of Majors in the Bush
and Minors in a rush
rise poets, write,

of Naira abscess
and numbing recessions
rise poets, write,

of rivers uncrossed
and leaders possessed
rise poets, write,

of coppers uncouth
and judges in soot
rise poets, write,

of buried traditions
and beleaguered mores
rise poets, write,

of basics backing off
and lecherous Reps
rise poets, write,

of peace displaced
and honour encased
rise poets, write,

of verse reversed
and poets disarmed
rise poets, write,

and of public dreamers
raising a song for commoners
rise poets, write,

fight and bite
and die for price,
set kites to flight
and fife for life,
rise poets, write.

Hurry your meals of crumbs

hurry your meals of crumbs
and day-dreams
empty these dishes before you
of lean hopes in main course
then chew your jaws to rhythms of agony
in this curse of a final course
for the times are not any softer
with this confinement to emergency wards
and choruses of groans for stillbirths
     from labour wards
     how many ribs for penury
     how many patches of watery stool
     for malnutrition
     how many registers
     for unemployment, armoured robberies
     how many fires for tidying up
     discrepancies at the treasury
     how many tiers for slumbering finances?

so many how manies, spices
hurry that course then, the main
of fat frustrations and aborted harvests
and sip sour grapes for dessert.

Rebirth

I hurry to those drums
The summons to my beginnings
To stretch my creases
Distortions on my palm lines
Warped strokes of my progression
In time

My spirit strains inclined
And thirsty for fresher sips
And in this couch of unities
My fuses itch for rebirth
This dip to end the scorch
Of morning haze
Of mid-day clouds
And evening mists
Celestial mentors moderate my lines
And monitor my continuing

Labyrinths of my mind

I

I thought I caught a flicker of light
In the surrounding darkness
But now my perseverance must endure
For visions of my mind
To sketch the scapes of reality

II

I imagined the fires out
And ashes heaped up in my centre
Memories of a flame that once glowed
Was all I had left
But the cold ashes of a burnt urge
Now scald my palms
I catch another flicker
Beneath a buried beam
Proclaiming the resurrection
Of a dead dream

III

Like a prodigal
I return to the realms
Of sustaining grips,
My wandering spell cast away
I feel the loosened loops around my centre
Tightening
Cold snatches of lonely nights
Retreating
I retrace my steps
Down the alley of love

IV

I can see clearly now from this view
Window on the world
My irises reveal cornerstones
Of shelters buried beneath items
Classified 'RUBBISH'
I hurry the sharpness of my shovel
Into this heap for the golden block

V

Once upon a crazy moment
I turned my back on a shiny pearl
My eyes clouded in the mist
Of an after-storm inside me
Upon that shameful second
Shiny pearl was a grain
Of wasted dust
But the storm subsided
And in the light that followed
The pearl shone
Spotlights fall on my craze
And the shame of a misguided second

He gave me a poem to do it with

my muse came again with dawn today,
but i refused to hold hands
and talk about empty-headed soldiers on home-front
i refused to talk about demons and crazed zombies
who mortify democracy,
sergeants and lieutenants their mindsets
shunned by reason, their rulers warper
than Jack the Ripper's.
i didn't wish to think about drudgery
and hunger nor doomsday everyday

i bluntly asked him for a new deal
new songs for a change
songs like those of Wordsworth and Milton
lyrics that told of the beauty of nature
streams, woods cosy enough for spirits
to abandon celestial pads and roam,
fraternising with birds and bards
i asked my muse to surf the oceans and
ride sky-diving waves with me
so i could peep into the kingdom
the ultimate resting place of poets
i demanded a trip to the Lake
Yeats's Isle of Innisfree
to pick the tuneful sounds of lakewater
lapping edges of nature's peace
and on our way back a stop
in the desert for dessert,
— see the trails of Omar Sheriff
and the ruins of Italy
— get an inkling of the mystery of Ozymandias
embossed on the headplate of his tomb
these were all i wanted this morning
these were my soul's yearning

for a day with a difference
and i would not hold hands and
do his will, this guardian muse

then he touched me where it snaps my sanity:
BBC news-hour carried word
of fresh fires lit by rascals in a kangaroo court
Ken the choice game for their gallows
because he raised his village voice
and looked the jackal in the eye
i knew it was coming, yet my shock was rude
my muse watched for a while,
counted the wrinkles of anger on forehead
then named the options
the Lake Isle of Innisfree, Ozy's dessert,...
i chose to kick soldiers in the bum
jackass kings in the groin

he gave me a poem to do it with.

No bondage for verse masters

when the universe is reduced to a cubicle
six feet by six feet of space
and sovereignty is handcuffed
to the key rings of the Inspector of Prisons
let none feel pity for us
for it's ocasion for a banquet—
that the gods receive atonement
and a new ward to school

when the tone of their verdict
matches the stretch of life
let none mar our glory with a mood
for a greater universe is opened
to the souls of poets,
past the horizons
of their comprehension.
those who think they chain
our persons lack contemplation
of the destinations of our flights

whatever their ruling, they lose
for we create the mysteries
which visit their sleep as misery,
we plant and tend the thoughts
that rouse the saner world to revolt.
and if they're foolish to pass
their terminal verdict,
the joker in their deck of cards,
we return with an army
of unseen poets and hammer
their heads day and night
until they haemorrhage to hell
we feed their carcasses to history
as footnotes, ibids, and et ceteras

this is the dilemma of impostors
in statehouse,
this is the banquet puzzle
that ridicules unwanted royalty
messing with a tribe
of verse masters
for whom there is no bondage.

To uncoming toasts

We cleared our throats
Ready for the toast
To new reins at day break
But we got their crush
And all are lame now
We are struck sterile
And our throats are sore
Stifled dry by uncoming toasts
With the diversion at cock-crow
Another dark-night-long trauma

A call to dance

you said we must sing and dance
you said we were not to mourn
your passing, for our cause you said
will not go with you to Shalom Cove
we thought hard and agreed to dance
we cleared our throats prepared to sing

but now that the time is here
to grant your injunction
and rejoice for ritual acceptance
now they've given us cause
and wired our feet for cultured dance
we cannot hear the music
from the drums of fed gods
because we count our numbers
and find the troupe is dwindled by one, you

you ordered a song and a dance
of rejoicing and merry-making
to celebrate their castrated verdict
that much we were going to give
but brother ken, it's not our fault
that those who took your orders
came back with war songs
and riotous thunder
and we are forced to dance to tune
the dance of war
which you taught us as souza boys

we have taken the oath of blood
to dance the nursery of tomorrow's peace
into place, we are sworn
to force the curtain
and end this bizzare drama

of intoxicated soldiers
who dare the gods and the world
and must go down, down, down.

Pollutants and generals

pollutants and generals
bestride our world
starlets choke
and cannot grow
into full stars
because those who seized
yesterday's moon
pollutants and generals
cover our firmament
even now
their children on props
wait in the wings
for a dynasty
burnt out stars fall
the moon becomes too full
to be clasped,
in the ritual
true regents
dislodge
reins of tyrant dynasties
and wear crowns
of new full stars
in a sky graced by a new moon.

Aso Rock*

today,
cave-men live within your walls
removed from the civilising mission
of sense and sensibility
albeit by choice

you grant them grace of shackles,
a mountain fortress to shield
their treasure of confusion and rubble
as corrosive buffoonery flakes off
their wicked design on state

on our own part
we walk in the shadows
of your non-guilt condemned,
but we embrace this air in our minds
of freedom that sweeps past
your grounds beyond the reach
of your royal in-mates

on their part,
they pretend they lie in bliss, safe
but would rather truly
you were an open-air cathedral
and they didn't need the wall
of protection you provide
against poisoned arrows
dislodged by a nation debased

but they have sinned and come short
of the glory of *king*dergarten priests,
us on the lower rungs waiting
and dreaming the ceremonies
of change and ordination

but O rock of my vision's generosity
i cast you on a different stage
in a different time
and the way my spirit leaps
i know my vision awaits vindication soon

your reincarnation as the holied shrine
of faithful deities when your grounds
are cleansed of the gore
of cave-men playing presidents
propped up by brain-boosters
into overdrive, upside down.

then O rock, your insides will cease
to corrupt
then O rock, new tenants will raise
a virgin flag
then O rock, you will become
the true Rock
that enchants the world
with echoes of ancestral pride...

---

* Named after the Presidential Lodge in Abuja, Nigeria.

Ode to housemaster and swampmaster

(for my friends, Baba N.G. Ida and A.B. Acha)

i pick my pen
and scribble a thought
that weighs heavily upon my soul
you say i wield a gun
because my verse is the spotlight
that sets the crafty ablaze

i sing the songs on my mind
of themes around me
you say i blaspheme your office
because i chorus your ills
and remind the people of their itch

i write a secret letter
to you in our "Keep Off" Chamber
but your doorman uses my Solomon sheet
to wrap pancake and peanut
leftover of last night's banquet
yet you swear i do not consult

i whisper to my neighbour
about misfortunes of the shattered
link between the Street and State House
anchored to the Ivory Tower
before Your Royal Swineness came
you snap an order
for me to be put away because
i 'incite the people'
really, you ignite the people

Housemaster,
what would touch your heart

about the lot of your people
to stop your camouflage of smiles
at Assemblies?
when will you be free
from the sentence of your own conscience
to walk our streets without escorts?

Housemaster,
the people crumble under your weight
why do you impose additional foul
from your Home Front?
you do not look on their faces
but their forced grins say
one crazy-dent is enough fraud
in State House.

Swampmaster,
when will you stop ordering their silences
by rifle kiss
those rascals who point the patch
on your trouser seat?
don't you know we all see
but only court cowardice because
we doubt your rational judgement
in accepting constructive criticism?

Swampmaster
haven't you heard it said
that pen is mightier than sword?
didn't housemaster tell you that
the trigger does not glitter forever?
and that pork-faced undertakers
will come for your remains
when the hacking is done?

Housemaster, Swampmaster
what kind of lives you lead
to fear men alive and dead?

didn't your teachers tell you the
truth always crashes the shell
of its concealment and blows as wind to
expose the anal mess of disgraced generals?

Housemaster, Swampmaster
how did you miss the final entries
in the diaries of your uncles
Mussolini and Idi Amin?
Or you simply learnt nothing
taking history for a pack of fables?

i do not threaten you but you must be told
in the name of fairness that one day before long
the Principal will order your flags
to fly at zero-mast
lumberjacks will stay home
and excitement will submerge mourning
amongst your pupils
for you suffocate a nation's hopes.

Secondmaster

Secondmaster! Secondmaster!
i cried
i bid you let them go
let my people be,
but screams of 'not yet'
crowd my eardrums drowning
the living songs of Firstmaster,
songs of promise
and first covenant

Secondmaster! Secondmaster!
i wailed
wear a human soul
let the children grow
but Secondmaster seeks to roast
my grain of wit
to silence the prophet
even before signposts
of rods, serpents and plagues
celestial wrath
ancestral anger

Secondmaster! Secondmaster!
i pleaded
ovations have died
rations have dried
but Secondmaster thinks only
of Geneva chest
deaf to dirges raised
in starving households
turning nation into a bush of ghosts
nightmares and haunts

now my grain of wit is weak

bashed by State Security
but Secondmaster must know
a threatened grain in flight
is a thousand germinations enroute
raising nations of compassionate
patriots for a continent in grief
who on return flights
make barbecues of roastmasters

Secondmaster must know
that a roving wit with
gory tales turns sympathisers
into undertakers for
unstately heads in the wake
of Uhuru's new songs
        songs of rebirth
        songs of promise
        christened by Firstmaster
        and chorused by growing disciples
        will smother sterile screams
        of 'not yet'
        before the coronation of Uhuru.

The dogs of Baidoa

daily
my innerwards turn
at the ghastly
sight
of their savagery
on kith and kin

these dogs of Baidoa
court my hate
with their bumper
health and crease-free
suits
besides kinsmen
on death row
chest bones, skulls and all
covered with thin slices
of death satin skin

dogs want to be
presidents in Baidoa
but do they have
courage to sit over a
parliament of ghosts?
   for their clansmen
   have departed in hunger
   starved beyond the
depths of catacombs
they raise a voice
for the union of the dead
some day soon
the whirl of enraged spirits
unearthed will choke
the barking dogs
of Baidoa
and castrate their dreams.

Like a rat

i have become like a rat
stalked by the king cat
i am the grasshopper on the lawn
that village rascals desire
for dessert
but if you are there
lord of the skies
in papa's songs to our infant ears
i crawl on broken knees
and cry my woes from the hollows
of a broken being
grant my supplication
stay me from the paws of those
who seek to barbecue my frail limbs
this eve of my coronation.

Pellets and bars

They're not in my gene
But triggers and pellets make me numb
Iron gates and cells knock me dumb
I have seen an eyeful
I have heard an ear's worth
If these gags would slip
I would pour my heartful
Of treated dung turned costly pearls
Purulent aid for revolting farmlands
Aiding this timeless passage
Of bags and packets of treasury bonds
    Of crickets hinting the loot
    Of currency in diplomatic bags
    Echoed in distant Heathrow,
    Of universal embargoes on jetties
    Making cement merchants of soldiers,
    Of much more than absent meals
    And strangled employments,
    Of governments and crap governors
    Expensive shitheads on butts
    My trap would rap
    But pellets and bars
    Make me dumb.

I shall sing my own song

(for a nation that hopes)

I shall sing my own song
In my time
These faultering steps would cease
And shivers of my muscles
Will marry the rhythms from my drum
I shall select my costume
Of pearls and ostrich feathers
Of cowries and fluffy cow tail
And when the curtain parts
And I take the stage in its beam
I shall blink for the world to film
A live one in the boom of fullness
This cold will go
This crack will heal
And I shall sing my song before long

Booths and thumbs

Let all who witness
Chorus my feral songs
Give pitch to the cleansing dirge
It is my valediction for the bulls of greed
Werewolves and numb visioners
Who must roost in haunted sepulchres
When we strip them of our ballot

Let all who fast
And desire to starve no more
Prosecute and judge
Castrate the claws of maiden mandates
Unroot the thickets of the Second Ballot
And fantasise of new dispensations

Orunmila* you rove in regal majesty
You see all and know all
It is you who decides
Who must live
And whose coverlet must be latent soil
Hearken and extend to them
Who desire your numinous guide
Executing the rites of booth and thumb

---

* Orunmila is a Yoruba deity.

In the nudity of rebirths

nude
i tread on punctured heels
ripping the shores
for cycles of time
seeking
platforms of rebounds
for transmissions
total upliftment from septic circles
onto new pedestals
new planes
and a new essence
the flavour of exile

nude
i ponder on our nation's lot
lost in the grips of barrel brains
and looters, concealed
in the caps i longed to wear
growing up
but not anymore because they
wear it, these jokers
dishonourable heads
who preside over our demise

nude
i imagine a nation reborn
along paths rid of displaced
roots, factors in the first
and several falls
but this is only my mind
travelling the paths
for a nation distressed
yet the ritual of rebirth
does not begin until

all will as one
it isn't complete without
libations of blood

in my nudity
i cannot catch the voices
of volunteers
and the priest must catch
the last train soon.

Jerry's town

I stumbled on a coven summit
And saw revelation splashed in red
The sombre sobriety of unquiet times
Diagnosed by pious sorcerers and loutish priests

Jerry's town will flick discordant chords
On cramped strings of atonal lyres
Manic specialists will swing to raucous tunes
In bandit-floated banquets
Peacelessness and queer wailings
Will stir the jinns of diamond mines
And ghosts of emptied nugget deeps
To belch and consume
Until the roaming architect
Headservant of her infancy
Is duly canonised
Not all the trigger flushings
Into catacombs of the unsung
Nor day-dreams of well-meaning fools
Will prune these distempered rants
Jerry boys must roam exotic streets
Hewers of wood
Until these stables are purified.

This hovering curse

This hovering curse
is not of motionlessness
but of drifts, directionless

rafts of three logs then four
then twelve, now
nineteen and a centre
yet clamourings for more
by those who would
be governor inside Statutory
coves, bugs of dissension
tear rafts apart
we wade in meadows of mutual
suspicion and muddied flows
of darkened rivulets drown
the drones of penitent
supplications for tranquilisers
for we murder sleep
and are restless as we drift

inspired chroniclers will
scribble in perpetuity
these lamentations
of impossible rafts
and directionless drifts
spineless heads and Heads
without reason, cataracts
on our troubled flows

when your trunk
and mine have fattened worms
below ground level, the new day
will scorch the beds of final rest
for the curse we incurred
on our innocent nation.

Curly waves

Curly waves sketch serrated shadows
On the brinks of my sanity
In the break of new confusion
Chaff and grain muddle in my vision
Modelling trains and brawns atwined
And I cannot tell one from the other
Scattered images running the furrows
Of my cognition
Wherefrom, whereto I am empty
Yet I strain to fathom these clouds
For what their later intentions
Shattering storms or showers of peace
Riddles and puzzles lock like
reindeer horns as I retreat into my shell
For another night of dreams
Of hopes for the unfolding of clouds.

Wipe your tears

yesterday again
the grass was cut
on execution ground
so, we know the Tribunal
has dressed another in golgotha robes

mothers wipe your tears
and seal the furrows on your faces
rivulets
of the harrowing pain within

salted overflows of anguish
do not stop courier kids
running risks of mid-day demise
pushing white snuff
in carts fuelled by giant Generals

your sons walk in the shadows
of people of 'grace' untouchable
in State[ly] House
and are caught in their web
of want and greed

first, second and endless tiers
at stock exchange, futile queues
at job bureaus
dress dinner tables with roasted hunger
in onion sauce
and between sleeplets, flights
and visions of banquets, jaguars
and porsches conclude the rites
of initiation

mothers, wage a war of curses, naked
crowd the ears of dawn
with the mouthful names
of Powder Lords masked
by your children's frames

those who deserve bereavement
must harvest mourning in lorry-loads
big bad names must burst with their
bubbles in Bangkok, Lagos and Bogota

mothers, wipe your tears
to clear your vision
so that when the grass is cut again
on execution ground
you may behold Faces-behind-the-mask
in golgotha robes
adorning stakes schemed for your sons.

Through the mirror

i am an eye bogged by reflections
of a gory sort
from this curse before me

refractions sear through me
casting double foci
of things before and after,
the strain of pains tutor my pupil
in this mirror

i am doubly cast
as palmist and psalmist
i see thick dark lines on
the spread palms of my race
from before me
linking the Flood to this
plague of recessionary worms
etching out cliff edges
from which we drop
our breath

Tiennamen, Sarajevo, Goma
like time-posts framing the mirror
through which i look,
this curse before me.

but i am doubly cast
the psalmist sees my chords
in fresh extension, another
phase, intoning beyond
cliff edge threat
of lean windows
for persisting rays widening

to cover a falling Wall in Berlin
setting borders to Arafat's Strip
on a human face arriving
in South Africa breaking fetters
on Nelson's wrists and ballots
my race leans on tomorrow,
crushing enemy worms.

The vanquished

the curtains rise revealing
settings of internal crisis,
but from these fringes
i hear the croak of man
derobed of grace and essence,
and behold the gust of ghosts
clamber out of mass graves
abused by the elements in Mostar
making their war internal to our world

nations witness the dismemberment
of state and soul
spread sorrow in Vitez
and bemoan the pinch
of fetters on the wrists
of embryonic nations.
sterile resolutions dress
the hinges of a crumbling centre,
harsh pills for a spangled world
beyond the scapes of Bosnia.

many are held hostage audience
of a macabre denouement,
blood and faith, tusslers
for parameters of nationhood,
bubbling cities to rubbles
deserted villages unfathomable
to a thousand goldsmiths
are scenes for a diminishing cast.

but complicity creates hostages
of a different kind,
hostages to Conscience.

we watch in silence
those who arm Bosnia's camps
from our ranks
lay wreaths of grass in Akabar
as the siege of Sarajevo sizzles
in charitable villainy.
heroes are made of casualties,
their past and future
consumed in the present,
under U.N. supervision, some say
perhaps rightly

in the end, audience or actor,
man remains the vanquished
fallen from glory
in the re-enactment of tragedy
on our mobile stage.

A Bosnian epitaph

(For all those buried in Bosnia's mass graves)

passer-by reading this epitaph
do not be misled by its rudeness
to think that Balkan culture
frugally marks its graves
to invest the spirits within
with reverent modesty

if we had a say,
and I speak for a whole community
tractor-heaped into this crowded
restlessness above which you stand,
we'd have opted for a separate
headstone to each of our names.

we had different sensibilities,
different thoughts
of life and death,
more than this horror
has space to reflect.
although you look around now
and think you see desolation
there's congestion beneath

and we're angry.
we would like to go in peace
resigned to our fate of victimage
but this jam impedes our going.

the silence you observe
disappears at dusk when we
seize the killing field hunt down
the guilty who have strayed
demolition squads and looters

of souls
no use for your world
no use for ours either.

passer-by you have strayed,
but stumbled upon a truth
concealed in Dayton.
take word back and seek redress
at least clear this jam
to release our shackled dignity
a separate headstone each
our modest request.

now you know our plight
a heavy price sits on the heads
of those who court sinful silence
and displease the restless dead.
hurry now, before the agitated
in our company break the truce
your gentle spirit earned.

Bosnian carols

"reports of overnight shelling
have just reached us from Vitez
Sarajevo's silent night was pounded by mortar
from surrounding hills
This is the BBC Monitoring Service
Early Morning News"

carols of a different kind
clutch the air waves
of a sick world on December 25

i peer out into the street
but my eyes are shut
to its emptiness and cold
the music from houses reaching
my ears drop hints of Santa's incarnates
gracing dinner tables
family fires, trees and heavy-breasted turkeys
awaiting the carving knives of those
to whom Christmas comes
those who witness The Birth
and for whom FM Radio carols

from an angled glimpse in the mind
i see folks in flight
fleeing from fired homes
journeying away from kindred roots
the cord that binds
leaving litres of blood
in trail to congeal in wintry clime
a Christmasless tribe shunned by Santa

and as my shutters close
i ask

when will Charity destroy their guns
and soothe angry nerves?
when will their Christmas return
with carols and turkeys
to end our doles to them

perhaps when my shutters close
again before another winter?

Bosnia's war

sperms have lost life
and become bullets,
lethal dicks the barrels
from which they're fired
making every man a warrior, armed
every woman, a moving target
in Bosnia's war

body-bags and broken limbs
no longer count the toll
new lives unanchored, unwilling
mothers starting indecent descents
scars for another generation
stain testimonials of Un-united Nations
in Bosnia's war

whistling shrapnels, racing rockets
serenade the brutality of cocked guns
as savage screams and groans
drown orgasmic drones
hurrying women in droves into buffers
manned by the beasts
in Bosnia's war

mass rape in the arsenal
of Bosnia's warlords. the rest of us,
accomplices in observer robes
count their dead and children of war
like demographers of doom.

There are no heroes

Dateline, April 1994
the world turned its back
on Kigali
making way for a carnage

the tooting was loud
and clear, the Tutsis
were fouled, harangued
but we wore blindfolds

the continent grew dark
before our eyes trained
only for Safari trails
and nature watch

we missed the hooting too
of Hutus on the run
bludgeoned at home
in the chase, infants
and infantries mauled
in millions floated with streams
bloated and angry in death

now they've fought their war
and diminished their lot
we hurry back to claim victory
of a population check

we see heroes in ourselves
mercy people
source of their aids
and in fact their LIVES!

we sit in judgement
over genocide but we ourselves
are party to the crime
of witness, guilty

so, ladies and gentlemen
let us fold our maps
and get out fast before angry
ghosts visit our courts
for there are no heroes
only actors and accomplices,
them and us.

On the shell of a dream

on the shell
of a dream
my name
on songs for a tribe
disturbed

on their lips
of goodwill
my dream
hemmed to night clouds
breaks into day
clear

on a podium
beyond dreams
the unities
i've always sung
penury and plenty
mashed
raise a lullaby
for a troubled world.

We clutch our dream

as seasons go, the last
is buried in tense, simple past.
only memories remain
of silhouettes cast
across a suffocating moon bogged
down by the weight of centuries

there on the mound sat Sipho
as we broke stones everyday
for letting our veins
surge with dreams of amandla.
but now tribulation is pilloried
and strung to winds hurrying off
across seas laden with sentiments
labelled 'yesterday'.
as seasons come, the current
is smeared with olive palliating
the sores of the last

season of glittering skin wrapped
in regenerative clouds
and opening up pores for fresh rains
to soothe the beds from
which new buds will rise

we clutch our dreams in our palms
our soul, a protective coat
as our breath hums gently
"osisi keleli Africa".

Dance of the gods

through the easy ears of night
i gather the checkered tones
of ancestral calls, rumbling drums
set the keys of buried decades
in our re-marriage to roots
roots disengaged along routes
in the bastardy of fake orientations
anniversaries of our baptism
in whitening solution in the hands
of priests with machine souls.

my mind's stage recast and the curtains
drawn, black roots people
the scenes moving to ancient tunes
off the drums of unseen drummers
and like spells cast by angered priests
i behold an audience in plea
begging the protocol of re-initiation
a thousand hands and a thousand tongues
stretching out of black sweaty frames
like the several fingers of an octopus
in search of the essence

but these are the dance steps of ritual
rebirth, dance of our ancestors
for among my people
the dance of ancestors
is the dance of the gods, the dance of life
and the covenant of ages.

'Isn't it ...?

isn't it amazing
that after all the high-culture
of swing and jazz,
the president goes into
the little room
and does ordinary people's things
like wee and poo-poo?

isn't it perplexing
that after all the pomp
of the cat-walk
super-models breathe
and succumb to cramps
like all other girls?

isn't it confusion
after all the stardom and highs,
society's heavyweights drop
polish to rape private things
and public vaults
like any other rogue?

isn't it so amusing
that after all the verse and jive
we all go away most times
same as we came
dropping velvet for the rags
of our coming, not one bit richer?
but isn't it all so human?

Vanity rose

Your sepals unfold
Caressed by the radiance of morning rays
Made up with the plumes of prime.
This captivating glow
Of your pollen dust
Ever tempting charm
Who, chancing along this path
Would not stop to pick or stroke
And display their find in public galleries?
But beggars are unmounted
For wishes and Horses run parallel courses.
Yet you swing unreservedly
To symphonies orchestrated
By several winds,
With each a different step
And a different secret
You prostitute your franchise
And watch a nation floundering
Your vanity breaks me
Several-master Rose.

This is the night

the shell is cracked
and its content in full glare
we know this is the night
that screws the blaze of a nation's sun

for us tomorrow withers
in this grope for receded light
our lot crushed under this pebble
that has grown into a boulder
before our eyes

through this night we must behold
the sweat of ancestral toil
awash in stagnant ponds, wasted
visions of our forebears
shredded like grandpa's farm overalls
and petals of our flowery growth forecast
now squashed in mid-season

but the days of miracles
are not yet over
the priest preaches every Sunday
so this boulder's speed may soon be clogged
when the plain unsteeps its mountain roll
our hopes suffer decay
but in the day of miracles
our faith may turn into mortar
that blasts heady boulders
and fashions fresh beginnings
beyond their exit
making us witnesses
to new seasons.

Our head

day breaks anew
but his head has reached menopause
our Head complains of brain thrush
his reasoning clogged

so are fibres of nationhood torn,
shredded by the recurring ignorance
of people in power
men of valour self-proclaimed
caught in trance
in palours far from their towers
sterile

and we have become
like sheep without a shepherd
roaming wide beyond our fields
and rummaging for pasture
in thorns and rubbles of state
awaiting another dawning
that's taking its time in coming

The solution

in times of desperate anger
and blistering desire for endmissions
only one solution soothes my soul

epidemic of ebola in the household
of uninformed heads
those who have
run
       out
       of
space
on

shoulders and breastplates
wearing epaulettes
of blood and guilt,
numerous
years of self-reward
for cowpea manouvres
and treasury
ambush
— our brigadiers
and generals—
    snuffed
    and cuffed
by ebola
many in our ranks
are hurt enough
to ponder the *karma*kazi
    and its final glory.

Songs of a peripheral monk

the weaverbird weaves nests in exhibition style
for a look and a nod for its skill
the woodpecker hollows out a shelter for itself
from fat tree stems, stamp of privacy
the redneck takes suicidal its plunge and nods
congratulations for self-accomplishment

but as a singer I sing the songs
of a peripheral monk, my lyrics
dynamite in the household
of prime time rogues, nuts whose
psychiatrist died long before their birth
and so every song for me is like a final
breath, relished like none before it
echoes reach their highest crescendo
launched from the cutting edge
from where no rednecks dare to leap,
that is sterner stuff
my tribe of peripheral monks
thrives on the edge!

What to do?

(For Ken Saro-Wiwa on hearing The Sentence)

now it's slightly too *chili* for upright
subjects on this platform, this front

a draught has started
from the mass of posters
we hoist to the world
that rides beyond our station
in commuter trains headed
for Erutuf, the city of lights

our folks are shivering
the messages into ripples
too fast to decipher from
electric trains blowing more draught

on to our stage in genocidal Shell
shielding an army of locusts

but what to do
if brethren crying for country
draw death-long sentences, cleft,
making life ungrammatical?

smear locust faces with faeces
of locust bean and dare their tribunal

to make me a sentence six feet deep?
or dive for the couch my wife has laid
beyond their reach in distant Berkshire?
i cannot break this date, too late
my soul haemorrhages for country

errand boy to guardian gods
i wait for my claws and a red pen
to knit the infelicities of their structures
into strangle cords for fatal conclusions, theirs

this, my humble calling
until spirit cobras feast on generals
until country leaves Erehwon
the city of darkness, permanently.

Rabbits and cats

the mind journeys in directions
unpre-determined when the self
dawdles
inside, the idler's
dreams are anchored distant from
lifelike portraits on a wall
in a tale of boredom

and so a bored rabbit
on fantasy trip grows out of its
minuscule coat and dons the spot
of leopards and the mane of lions
scuttles back and forth
believing itself to prowl,
roars in a fashion
audible only to its own mind
as mega-decibels befitting
big time games.

in the fuzzy retreats of rodent mind
reality merges with the intangible
in a game called 'SUICIDE'
the rabbit stands akimbo along path
of mastercats and whiskers
its dream tribe and medium
for a horrid conclusion
one concern on its mind-plate
philosophically magnanimous

"the physically endowed of the forest
must do more to protect under-privileged
kin from the assault of aliens!"
large heart of a small game
goes out to King Cat and starts

we th th eeeeeeeeeeeeeee"
but the claws of princely cubs
seal off rodent hallucinations and
suffocate a plea
for the forest's weak

beyond suicidal illusions
rabbits and cats
scuttle and prowl
in different packs squeaking
and roaring as tribes not one.

Clouds

they come in different sizes
small, medium, large and XL sheets
of cloud board up the heavens
concealing quarters of deliberate-ing gods

clouds come in differing shapes
and so the gods they shroud
big clouds, big gods
small clouds, small gods
thick clouds, macho gods
thin clouds, anaemic gods

all in all their decisions reach us
sometimes, as gentle breeze
conveying goodwill.
other times, storms and thunder
telling of cups full to brim
beyond legal limit

when the tongues of concealed gods
extend beyond clouds, their sheath
to lash us as torrents of rain
and blinding lightning
then it ceases to matter
what shape or size clouds take

our mortal frames too frail to bear
the brunt of godly anger ˙
even of thin clouds and anaemic gods.

Exile songs

every day now i hear a music
different from all around me,
one fit for my exile ears
i ride the buses on Dublin roads
but the tar runs past Ojota
in the direction of home.

in the silent cruise of the trans-island
coach, i hear the motor boys of home
screaming 'one more, one more passenger!'
low-tones coaxes in gaelicised English
settle like pidgin upon my senses

when the Angelus sounds
i hear it as music in the voice
of a distant Imam summoning faithfuls
to the 4 o'clock
yet i see no gourds and no ablutions
and no spotlessly clean robes fit
for the presence of God

even the billboards
are in on this giant conspiracy
hoisting pictures of Herzegova spotting
the Wonderbra and a quizzical smile
teasing 'are you game lads?'
yet i behold not her splendour
splashed upon the billboards
but familiar bosoms
with a different statistics
rolling to the rhythm of girdles and beads
imagination and recollections explode
to billboard size

it's no madness, it's nothing strange
just a plague of exile songs
playing on the discman of my soul
far from those who share the rhythm
of my roots.

A letter to cyril in Indianapolis

my dear Cyril
    zombies have scratched
    the itch on fore-finger
    against the rough protrusion
    on barrel skin

    the canons have spilled
    and smeared the stakes
    with the redness
    of their extinguished essence
    those who stole Sunday 22nd April
    to adjust the scale
    or break shaky rafts

    many yet may smear
    and many may fall
    if the dragon nets
    entangle human frames on the run
    in this mad search
    or harvest of vengeance
for me home-front no longer holds promise
except waves of valediction
wafting closer as September comes
drifting my dreams to shores away from home.

Who chewed the kurd?

the horror gale is spent
streams of blood dammed,
desert storm has gone to ebb
but dusts of fury hang still
this day of reckoning

we all know that sheep in graze
devour their grass
and chew the cud
for another meal,
but who chewed the Kurd
for dessert
after the ritual of crossfires
on desert sand?
who urged Kurdish guts
to tempt the Norman's Stag
and erect slaughter slabs
down mountain slopes
for their race?

speculators and rumour mongers
have spoken their fill
but those who know
must tell chroniclers
for tomorrow's race
whose voice it was
that rang through a sandy Bush
hurrying the Kurd to conclude
ceremonies of castration on the Stag
without the carver's knife
for that indeed is he
who chewed the Kurd.

Times like now

i am but one david
without a sling
before a thousand goliaths
in stampede

its times like now
i find i need no
Chambers to spell out FAITH
for i soar so much
i'm proud of me
and the owner of my wings.

Of contingency votes

on the counter of Geneva
stately fingers drip
leaving prints big enough
for Intelligence clues
of the alien nest
of last year's contingency votes
and the twistedness
of statesmen in the hood

but only the unintelligent
bite fingers of benevolence
only the hard of reasoning
miss their benefactor
in an identity parade
and thus this infliction
of blindness and of silence
at the Intelligence Unit
is worrying

for they scan the air space
over Sydney when looters
congregate in money halls
in Geneva
our operatives suffer a squint
in addition to their dumbness
because our generals have
a formula for fear,
the change of guards

but we are not frustrated
because we know
quakes rupture the earth
and gold-diggers vanish
with the tremors that come before,

soon our taxes will sit in judgement
and make carcass for hounds
of Geneva pilgrims emptying treasuries
and inflict cricket brains at the Unit
with verbal diarrhoea
unwearing their squints
to probe alien nests
of Contingency Votes.

Rotten eggs and doublespeak

Dele Giwa
Pa Alfred Rewane
Kudirat Abiola
Shehu Yar'Ardua
And many more
Forced encores
Unpleasant

innocents on the inside
done in by a 'shitstem'
    whoever served rotten eggs
    as main course to the Bench
    must now fumigate
    courtrooms of uncivil gas

    whoever tutored coppers in doublespeak
    to the ridicule of clownish wigheads
    must now preside over ceremonies
    of sanitisation at Aso Rock

    or who does not know
    that rotten eggs and doublespeak
    are recipes for the broth of chopped justice
    logs in the eye of a nation?

Season of tribulation

we're far into the season of tribulation
and we await the dawn
that will sponge us clean of this spell of damnation
we wriggle and writhe in fetters of bondage
and our droplets of blood upon droplets of sweat
work the mines in Jo'burg
to sustain an overwhelming minority

our snapping muscles tend the greens
but balls of hot lead are the windfall apples
we pick on township streets

our sweat farms the sweet
that intoxicates and sets racist blood on fire

the discriminations we thought were transient passions
bound to be carried away like firewood smoke
on the wings of changing winds
have borrowed robes of permanence

and this morning in Pretoria
there'll be a mass burial
i hear there'll be a Mass before interment for them
black brothers and sisters
in want of a seat in council
and those who yearned to live
working at the factory in Cape Town
permanently silenced

still their radio toasts to further doom
'new policy of monitoring black population:
black-white ratio must be bridged'
'afrikaans for instruction'
and Soweto's children are led to the slaughter
visitations of their fathers' iniquities?
but unto how many generations more?

we were harried on the streets of Sharpville
we were brutalised
and now we know like our fathers before us
that the season of tribulation is the season of castration
and black the colour of tragedy for now

because we denounce 'Whites Only'
on farmlands of our forebears we're battered
we're mauled for afrikaans
in our preference for the melody in Bantu
we're caged for breaking their law
their curse of sterility
but we multiply by Supreme Essence

and extend the ratio by Divine Blessing
we're garnered at hell gates on Robben Island
and smothered in the cells of Jo'burg

but we shall return
and raise cyclones and tornadoes
to twist the spine of racism in a wild spiral

even as we lie belly-flat in trenches
and carry our cross in the streets
our aspirations are coffins for apartheid
our hopes, dirges for racism
so let us clear our throats for the toast at dusk
a toast to the glory of mankind
for tomorrow at dawn
the streets shall be loud with victory songs
celebrating new liberties and dignity
with the flags lowered in Pretoria
of deprivation and of segregation
of depression and of discrimination
to end our season of tribulation

Pamberi Nachirimenga, Pamberi
Forward with the revolution! Forward.

When the sun goes to roost

tonight when the sun goes to roost
freedom bugle will rent the air
and all who rise for mankind
will raise a mighty camp fire
for a midnight feast
and the streets will be heavy
with the breath of martyrs on the rounds

but for all who deal by colour
tonight will be worse than at Passover
for though bugles rend mountains
and take the veld to task
the bird of night will block their eardrums
with grains of corn and deafen them
to songs of new hopes

tonight when the sun goes to roost
some hands must be on deck
for the duty at dawn
the left overs of our passover feast—
pass laws, education bills, colour bars
must course their journeys with the Limpopo
and the carcasses of routed racists
must wind and stretch with the Orange flow

tonight when the sun goes to roost
and the ritual of cleansing begins
ex-convicts and their jailors
programming our passover feast
will rid the laws of shame and hate
for a fresh start at dawn
changing scapes will show
doors of council chambers fly open
to previous 'degenerates' in the **majority**

allowing popular mayors in Jo'burg and Pretoria
and consecrating Robben Island for tourists

when the sun goes to roost tonight
our spirits will wear new garments
and be lifted in the frenzy of liberty feast
this ritual before the dawn of our great expectation
this feast of pass over of all power to the people.

A season of new full moons

the harp is resouled and the music changes
to the amazement of all but the spirits
of those who propel windblasts
to unveil fresh trails
for a season of new full moons

the harper's persistence
has twisted the flutes of dissension
bugle summon to arm
and solo performers leave in lonely
boxes willed by the mass
clearing the stage for a symphonic
orchestra, inspired voices
have found a new song to serenade
their season of new full moons.

slip slap against the wind
crossroads have folded up
for a colourless highway
streams of people, yesterday's warriors
crawlers in trenches have clinched
the prize in Oslo sharing a glory
for long cocooned in toxins brewed
in camps of hatred
bottled for one time enemies
redefined as compatriots in a search
for new histories in tomorrow's books
        theirs is the glory of new full moons

        the gaping wounds of centuries
        have reincarnated as fresh visions
        for a distressed tribe relieved,
        as the harper strings new notes conjuring
        washwaters for cleansing, hoisting smiles

on the faces of previous sorrows

bridegrooms have found willing brides
and their bands of union glitter
in the songs floated by harpers
and chorused by a mixed orchestra
in a symphony to new full moons
in Azania.

Portraits

Hanging out in the mist of time
On the rugged walls of an eerie future
Splashed in the colour of gold
I peer at them
Portraits of coming blossoms,
These dreams and fancies
Fastened now to webs in darkrooms
Will rear tomorrow's light
When faggots of our present bane
Sprawl fumigated in spillages
When stretches of revolting greens
Usurp patches of acrid barrenness
Antlered groins will snap austere bands
Gold-edged portraits breaking out of shell
Will leap into morning rays and blaze.